NO GOD-FREE ZONE:

Understanding the Presence of God

By Adrian N. Stovall

Copyright © 2014 by Sacred Covenant Ministries

ISBN: 978-0-9768335-2-9

All rights reserved. No part of this book may be reproduced in any form, except for the inclusion of brief quotations in a review, without written permission from the author.

Unless otherwise indicated, Scripture taken from the New King James Version®. Copyright © 1982 by Thomas Nelson, Inc. Used by permission. All rights reserved.

Other Scripture quotations from New Living Translation, copyright © 1996, 2004, 2007, 2013 by Tyndale House Foundation. Used by permission; King James Version by Public Domain

This book is dedicated to Pamela, my wife, who is my best friend and precious love of my life. I thank God every day for the gift and life-partner graciously given to me by Him.

Without Pamela's encouragement and tireless support, this work would not have been finished. Thanks for your ever present help that is only second to the faithfulness of Jesus Christ.

Foreword

A basic lesson most children are taught in Sunday School is that God is everywhere and He is with them. Somehow that lesson seems to get lost for some of us as we get older and face the issues of life that challenge our faith. However, in his book, *No God-Free Zone: Understanding the Presence of God*, Adrian Stovall reintroduces that basic message to us. He breaks down the 24 verses of Psalm 139 to remind us that not only is God everywhere, He is with *us* — wherever we are and loves us unconditionally.

This short but powerful book is one that should be part of the study library of every student of the Word. It is full of simple truths that will have a huge impact on its reader. As the wife of the author, I know what a labor of love this has been, and the fruit of that labor is a, potentially, life-changing narrative.

With many Scripture references, Adrian encourages us to remember that God is right where we are — even when we don't feel Him, when things don't go our way and when it seems our enemies are out to get us. He wants us to understand that the presence of God is something that we should desire and experience on a daily, moment-to-moment basis. It's not just for special people who have a special calling; it's for every person who names the name of Jesus.

Accepting His love, living in His love and walking in His love is recognizing His presence and the transformation that comes from knowing that God is always there. This book will inspire you to draw closer to God.

Pamela A. Stovall
Pastor, Author, and Co-founder of
Sacred Covenant Ministries

Contents

Foreword	iii
Introduction	vii
Chapter 1 You Know Me	1
Chapter 2 You've Got My Back	7
Chapter 3 No Hiding From You	13
Chapter 4 You Purposed Me	21
Chapter 5 Precious Are Your Thoughts	27
Chapter 6 My Enemies	33
Chapter 7 Test Me	41
Chapter 8 Living in God's Presence	47

Introduction

The concept or term "No God-Free Zone" was introduced in a book written by my wife and me, entitled *Marriage is Not For the Faint of Heart.* The thought conveyed in that book was that our homes and our families were not areas free from the loving intervention and control of God. In looking at the lives of people, it appeared as though they thought their homes were places where they were on their own or that the rules of Christian conduct were suspended. Many, erroneously, believe that marriage is a zone where brotherly kindness or patience is not required because this is their independent area of control and influence. The book addressed our need to allow God to be Lord of our entire lives, including our home and marriage relationship.

In this work, I want to continue discussing the expansive reach of the "No God-Free Zone" regarding our *entire* lives. Together, we will examine the truth of how God is not only sovereign but also interested and involved in every area, situation, thought, and endeavor that touches our lives. To make sure that we understand the inclusiveness of every area, I will discuss various zones of our existence that are open and available to God's loving touch.

Through the use of Scripture, with Psalm 139 as the foundational Scriptural theme, the understanding that

God cares about every area and issue of our lives—and leaves us to handle nothing by ourselves—will be presented. It is my prayer and goal to help you:

1. understand and believe that there is no aspect of life from which we should exclude God for any reason,

2. realize there is no task that God expects us to handle on our own without Him,

3. know in your heart that the love of God reaches, covers, manifests and dominates any and everywhere we are or are not.

May you have the peace of knowing that there is "No God-Free Zone", and God is not a liar. Hebrews 13:5-6 is God's promise to never leave us or forsake us. We can take Him at His word and discover, as others in the Word of God, that He who promised is faithful to deliver. Numbers 23:19 (NKJV) declares, "God *is* not a man, that He should lie, Nor a son of man, that He should repent. Has He said, and will He not do? Or has He spoken, and will He not make it good?" As we trust God, we will find Him more than willing and able to prove Himself trustworthy and reliable in every situation of life. There is no place where God will not reach and protect us if we seek and trust Him.

CHAPTER 1

You Know Me

Psalm 139:1-4

O Lord, You have searched me and known me. You know my sitting down and my rising up; You understand my thought afar off. You comprehend my path and my lying down, And are acquainted with all my ways. For there is not a word on my tongue, But behold, O Lord, You know it altogether.

In Psalm 139:1, David declared that God had searched him and knew him. In a world filled with so many people with whom we interact, I would propose that we often feel unknown and most of the time misunderstood. Humanity finds itself so intrigued with the lives of other people that we watch TV sitcoms and reality shows created about the relationships of strangers. Our desire is to gain some insight into who they are and how they live. We so often think about how we are perceived and whether others think the same way we do. It's the curiosity of wondering about the lives of the coincidental people we pass in cars or see walking on the streets around us. We ponder, "Do they have the same challenges and questions about life we have, how do they cope, and do they know God the way we do?"

Do those around us really know us? Do those we designate as closest to us, such as family, spouses, friends, and church family, really know our heart and the internal workings of our minds? With the many thoughts and decisions made each day in our minds and our lives, can we really say that *we* are even fully self-aware and conscious of whom we are? Despite the level of confidence we may exhibit in our answers to these questions, it is critical that we understand the extent of God's commitment to, and knowledge of, the intimate details of our lives.

As in every relationship, the more time spent in each other's presence, the deeper the understanding and assurance we have of the devotion to each other. And so it is with God. David spent time with God in prayer and worship and had developed an understanding of the depth of God's love for him, in particular, and humanity as a whole. The time spent with God gave David insight into God's pre-existing condition of unconditional love and commitment. I describe God's love as a pre-existing condition because it was God-initiated, independent of David's actions or mankind's. As we look into various Scriptures recording the relationships that godly men have had with God, we see that it is a record of what they came to understand as God's inescapable loving character.

Genesis 1:27 tells us that God created male and female in His image. God desires relationship with man and has reached out to establish and maintain a godly relationship predating the beginning of time. I believe that knowing that we are created in God's image allows us to understand some of our inherent desire to have a personal relationship with God and our fellow man. Our desire to know others, and be known by others, who are destined to touch our lives, produces an innate hunger to be understood based on who we really are internally and not from just a superficial, external presentation. Therefore, it is essential that we acknowledge, as recorded in Job 10:8 and Psalm 119:73 that God made and fashioned us. There is no closer relationship than that between Creator and creation. Human beings do not have the comprehensive ability to know each other's thoughts, intents, feelings, fears, desires, or true passions, but God does. God cares for us as no other human being can or ever will.

Psalm 17:3 records the prayer of David that expresses his understanding of God's intimacy with his life:

> *You have tested my heart; You have visited me in the night; You have tried me and have found nothing; I have purposed that my mouth shall not transgress.*

David was acknowledging that God did not make a cursory examination of him but probed deeply into the heart and darkness of his being for any obstacles to their ongoing relationship.

We find Jeremiah's thoughts regarding God's knowledge of him in Jeremiah 12:3:

> *But You, O Lord, know me; You have seen me, And You have tested my heart toward You…*

We need to be assured, in our hearts and minds, that God's Spirit searches our hearts to know us and to be available to help us in any situation.

God knows the secrets of our hearts and tells us that nothing can be hidden from Him. There can be no misunderstanding of our intents and agendas by God. God wants us to know that He knows us and remains committed to our salvation and promotion. He knows, and yet, has given His very best in Jesus Christ to address our greatest barrier to fellowship with Him: our sin nature. We cannot, and must not, attempt to hide from God and His loving character; for it is only through running to Him that we find redemption and release from sin, guilt, and shame. When we know and believe *He* knows, then we will be able to obey, and as 1 Peter 5:7 (NLT) says "Give all your worries and cares to God, for he cares about you."

To reinforce the fact that God knows and sees, look at these scriptures:

Jeremiah 16:17 *For My eyes are on all their ways; they are not hidden from My face, nor is their iniquity hidden from My eyes.*

Proverbs 15:3 *The eyes of the Lord are in every place, Keeping watch on the evil and the good.*

Psalm 33:13-15 *The Lord looks from heaven; He sees all the sons of men. From the place of His dwelling He looks on all the inhabitants of the earth; He fashions their hearts individually; He considers all their works.*

Job 31:4 *Does He not see my ways, And count all my steps?*

We may ask how well and comprehensively does God know us. God knows our thoughts before we think them. We can never surprise God or require Him to scramble to develop a new plan B based on our response to Him. Scriptures tell us that He knows where we are going and where we will stop. He is familiar with all our ways, and knows what we will say before we say it. To some people this is a little frightening. However, to those who know that God loves them, this is an expression and experience of overwhelming security in a world of uncertainty. Let's look at some other scriptures that confirm how intimately He knows us:

Psalm 94:11 *The Lord knows the thoughts of man, That they are futile.*

Proverbs 24:12 *If you say, "Surely we did not know this," Does not He who weighs the hearts consider it? He who keeps your soul, does He not know it? And will He not render to each man according to his deeds?*

2 Kings 19:27 *But I know your dwelling place, Your going out and your coming in, And your rage against Me.*

Job 31:4 *Does He not see my ways, And count all my steps?*

2 Chronicles 16:9 *For the eyes of the Lord run to and fro throughout the whole earth, to show Himself strong on behalf of those whose heart is loyal to Him. In this you have done foolishly; therefore from now on you shall have wars."*

Hebrews 4:13 *and there is no creature hidden from His sight, but all things are naked and open to the eyes of Him to whom we* *must give account.*

Proverbs 5:21 *For the ways of man are before the eyes of the Lord, and He ponders all his paths.*

Daniel 2:22 *He reveals deep and secret things; He knows what is in the darkness, and light dwells with Him.*

God knows our past, present, and future completely. He not only *desires* to know us, He *actually* knows us and loves us with an unconditional love that is beyond our comprehension. In the face of life's challenging circumstances, we must remember God has accepted us into His Beloved (Jesus) according to Ephesians 1:6 (NKJV) which says **"**to the praise of the glory of His grace, by which He made us accepted in the Beloved." When we face rejection in life, it is important to remember that God knows us and has accepted us in His family of the beloved.

God has created a world in which man is His crowning jewel of creation for His glory and fellowship. Man may desire to run from God, but God desires our company and designed our world so that it is impossible to enjoy the full benefits of His creation without Him. Truly, for mankind on this planet or universe, there is no God-free zone. There is no place where we can hide or remove ourselves from the loving presence of Jesus Christ's Father God. For those of us who have accepted the gift of God's love embodied in Jesus Christ, this is a truth that provides great comfort, assurance, and security.

CHAPTER 2

You've Got My Back

Psalm 139:5-6

You have hedged me behind and before, and laid Your hand upon me. Such knowledge is too wonderful for me; It is high, I cannot attain it.

Many of us have family members, spouses, or friends who may say to us that they have our back, but none can promise to secure our present or future. The declaration of having our back by loved ones is indeed a statement of support and commitment. The psalmist here, in verse five above, declares that God has beset, hedged, or hemmed him behind and before. The word hedged has the meaning of being protected, surrounded or bound, or limited in a way that may be described as boxed in. God not only hedged his present but also his future to assure that his life was and would be a triumphant success. This was a statement acknowledging the assurance of the care provided by God Almighty toward him and for us today as believers.

How exciting life can be if we believe in our hearts and minds that God has our interest, success, and safety so covered that we are described as being surrounded by His loving care. This is for us to know with confidence, that we are protected, not only for today but the future. The concept of being surrounded implies that every eventuality that may occur in our lives is under the loving purview and protection of God. In this case, the phrase "every eventuality" means complete and comprehensive coverage. Think about that for a moment, and run your list of fears and nightmare scenarios through your mind and realize that God has them all under control. WOW, wonder of wonders.

Let's look at a few scriptures where God's people acknowledged His protection:

Psalm 32:10 *Many sorrows shall be to the wicked; But he who trusts in the Lord, mercy shall surround him.*

Psalm 34:7 *The angel of the Lord encamps all around those who fear Him, and delivers them.*

Psalm 125:2 *As the mountains surround Jerusalem, so the Lord surrounds His people from this time forth and forever.*

God wants us to be confident in His devotion to those who accept Jesus Christ as their Lord and Savior. The psalmist in 139:6 indicates that the knowledge of God's all-inclusive protection is too wonderful and beyond true comprehension. Many people, today, share those same feelings of not being able to understand the full meaning and extent of God's love and promised care.

Our challenge is to believe God's Word and receive the peace and security that results from knowing God cares and is working for our benefit. We must be aware that God is always working for our good. We must pay close attention, and recognize the many manifestations of His intervention and nurturing orchestrations in our lives. If we truly believe that God has our back, there is no place we would want to go without Him or desire to not have Him included. In other words, we have "no God-free zone". God lives within us and will work for us if we believe Him to.

Here are some scriptures recorded regarding the ways of God:

Job 5:9 *Who does great things, and unsearchable, Marvelous things without number.*

Job 11:7 *"Can you search out the deep things of God? Can you find out the limits of the Almighty?*

Isaiah 40:28 *Have you not known? Have you not heard? The everlasting God, the Lord, The Creator of the ends of the earth, Neither faints nor is weary. His understanding is unsearchable.*

Psalm 147:5 *Great is our Lord, and mighty in power; His understanding is infinite.*

Romans 11:33 *Oh, the depth of the riches both of the wisdom and knowledge of God! How unsearchable are His judgments and His ways past finding out!*

Hebrews 10:23 *Let us hold fast the profession of our faith without wavering; for he is faithful that promised;*

One of Satan's greatest deceptive tactics is to provide false evidence that what God has said is not working and will never work. How many times have events occurred that, at first impression, predict failure; then God, who always has the last word, brings blessing and victory from what appeared to be certain defeat. The fight of faith is always to believe God's promises over all circumstances. Easily said, but true belief is founded in daily experiences where God works in our everyday lives to build relationship and give confident assurance in His faithfulness to us personally. God promised to never leave us or forsake us in Hebrews 13:5, and we must know and believe that He will not and *cannot* lie.

The fact that God has our backs, or best interest at heart, does not mean that we will never experience hardship or difficulties in life. The truth is that we learn obedience through our suffering, just as Jesus did. The times of growth that occur in our lives come mainly from the struggles while waiting on God to faithfully deliver on His Word. It would be deceptive to tell you that everything will proceed smoothly, but God promises to bless us so that we will be able to boldly say, "God is our Helper." If we trust and wait on the Lord, He will never leave us or forsake us so that we will boast and boldly declare His faithfulness.

An example of this principal is revealed in the book of Daniel where the account of the children of Israel's Babylonian servitude is told. The book of Daniel records what happened to them as a result of disobedience and rebellion toward God. The Israelites were taken from their homeland and forced to serve the Babylonians. Over and over again, as Daniel, Shadrach, Meshach, and Abed-Nego determined to obey God's Word in the face of threatened and real destruction, we see God delivering them from annihilation. The Hebrew boys were not transported out of Babylon but given victory in the midst of their situation or suffering.

In Daniel 1, we see where, in obedience to God, they challenge the dietary dictates of their captives and request a test to determine the healthiest diet. They emerged victoriously, appearing healthier than those not adhering to God's plan. This resulted in them being given more favor with God and their captors. In Daniel 3, Shadrach, Meshach, and Abed-Nego refuse to bow to the Babylonian idol god and are sentenced to death by incineration in a fiery furnace. The end result was a supernatural deliverance orchestrated by God with their lives being preserved and unbelievers being convinced of the protecting power of the Almighty God of Israel. In Daniel 6, we read where Daniel refused to stop praying to God, and he was thrown into a den of hungry lions. Daniel was required to stay in the den overnight but emerged unharmed, once again witnessing to the keeping power of his God.

In Acts 16, we also read where Paul and Silas are imprisoned for their ministry in Jesus' name, and God, again, showed up demonstrating His power of deliverance. In the examples cited in Daniel and Acts, there was deliverance in the midst of difficulty or suffering, proving God's faithfulness.

God has us hedged in before and behind. Dare to believe, and await His faithful deliverance in the midst—or through possible avoidance—of pain and suffering. The thing that we can be assured of is His deliverance of blessing to those who trust in Him as says Psalm 84:12: *O Lord of hosts, Blessed is the man who trusts in You!*

In the final analysis, we must be able to happily say with the psalmist that God has laid His hand upon us; and to know in our hearts and spirits that God is there for us; and His hand is more real and comforting than the hand of our spouses, family members, or friends. Have you ever watched a parent guide his child through a crowd with his hand on the child's head or shoulder? The protection and guidance provided only works as long as the child submits to the helping hand. It will always be our choice to yield to God's love or reject it. Seek and embrace the touch of God in your life. Those who yield and receive are blessed and thankful for God's manifested nurturing character.

CHAPTER 3
No Hiding From You

Psalm 139:7-12

Where can I go from Your Spirit? Or where can I flee from Your presence? If I ascend into heaven, You are there; If I make my bed in hell, behold, You are there. If I take the wings of the morning, And dwell in the uttermost parts of the sea, Even there Your hand shall lead me, And Your right hand shall hold me. If I say, "Surely the darkness shall fall on me," Even the night shall be light about me; Indeed, the darkness shall not hide from You, But the night shines as the day; The darkness and the light are both alike to You.

The psalmist, in these verses, was telling us that God is omnipresent in the sense of being ever-present and pervasive. In other words, there is nowhere that God is not present, interested, or sovereign. There is nowhere we can go physically or mentally that God's presence is not to be experienced. This is an important reality and concept for us to understand in order to take full advantage of God's gracious loving care. I'm sure you have encountered people who seem to believe they can hide from the presence of God. It's like the little toddler who thinks he becomes invisible when he covers his eyes. Scripture tells us that there is no hiding place for those who want to exclude God or those whom Satan tries to convince that their sins or failures prevent God from being ever-present. In other words, for those who embrace God, we are never beyond His reach or protection; and for those who wish to avoid or deny God's influence, the situation is the same. There is no hiding place or limits to the range of domain or span of influence for God Almighty.

We need to know that there is no responsibility, activity, or life experience on the face of the earth where God has said, "You are on your own with this. Good luck with that". People, many times, rise up in pride and try to bring their so-called accomplishments to God saying, "Look what I have done," or claim no need for God's assistance. Yet God desires to be in the center of everything that happens in our lives–EVERYTHING! We need to understand that we were created for God's glory, and we need to bring the glory of our lives back to God, in recognition of His sovereignty and demonstrated love. God refuses to share His glory with anyone else, but His grace and unconditional love are available to all who ask.

Isaiah 42:8 (NLT) *"I am the Lord; that is my name! I will not give my glory to anyone else, nor share my praise with carved idols.*

God has promised to be with us. Sometimes, though, we think about God the same way we do our loved ones. In other words, when they say they will be with us, there is no real assurance. Their desire is admirable and loving, but we can't really place our lives totally in their hands. Their ability to be there at all times is very limited. However, all throughout scripture, God has promised (and dares us to believe Him) to be integrous to His word.

Don't you know that our belief, trust, hope and faith in Him are the only things that are going to motivate God to act on our behalf? God has promised, but our faith in His word is what causes Him to move – not our need, crying, or pitiful situation.

Psalm 91:14-15 *"Because he has set his love upon Me, therefore I will deliver him; I will set him on high, because he has known My name. He shall call upon Me, and I will answer him; I will be with him in trouble; I will deliver him and honor him.*

Isaiah 41:10 *Fear not, for I am with you; Be not dismayed, for I am your God. I will strengthen you, Yes, I will help you, I will uphold you with My righteous right hand.'*

Where You Are He Is

Our home is the place that we describe as our castle or where we rule and think we are supposed to be in control as lord and master of our domain. God wants to help, and He awaits our invitation for assistance in managing our homes and families. Even though God desires us to have our homes in godly submission, nowhere does He tell us to handle it on our own. The critical ingredient for God's intervention, regarding any need, is our personal request for His involvement. He will provide supernatural insight and discernment into the issues and concerns of our challenges. Our home can become a place for our families to receive and disseminate God's wisdom regarding life. Our homes are an opportunity to provide a safe place to understand and experience the loving protection afforded to those who receive, trust, and obey God's redemptive plan.

Schools or training centers are where we go to be educated beyond our present capabilities, or knowledge. This is fertile ground for God to manifest His promise-keeping power. To know that God is present to aid in the expansion of every area of life (our godly behavior, character, parenting, work skills, and life-survival skills), should bring comfort and give us great confidence in our eventual success. God wants us to be knowledgeable and informed so that He may also assist us with our personal and spiritual growth.

We must know that God is an untiring source of insight, ability, and creativity for those who trust Him even at work where proficient skill execution and favor are needed daily.

In our community, God shows up to help us decide where to live and how to allow Him to shine through us as a representative and witness to His glorious power, working within us. We should believe that God has placed or will place us, and allow us to follow His great plan for our lives under the cover of His assuring presence.

At our places of fellowship with God and the Body of Christ, He will guide us in deciding where to attend and how to get involved. Provision will be made for learning how to interpret God's Word, hear His voice, and then obey in the timing and designated location of His providence.

If we look, we will see God in private moments and locations where we may feel alone and perhaps hidden from the rest of world and our friends. Be confident that God will never leave us alone or forsake us. God lives within the believer and is ever ready to assure our success in following His plan. At those times in our life when we don't appear to hear from God, and we are waiting on Him; when we feel intensely needy and anxious for God's confirmation or perceived directive, this is the time we must trust that God knows who and where we are at all times. In what may seem to be a dry season of life, where we think that we are somehow abandoned due to our current situation, God is not hiding from us, and we can't hide from Him. He is there, ever faithful. Even in those times of disappointment and failure that we thought would never occur (or would never repeat itself again); or when we let others down and they us, we are still never alone.

Conversely, on the mountaintop of life, when seemingly everything is going our way and we don't want the moment to end (and yet we fear it will), know that God is orchestrating our lives and is not going to leave us.

We may deal with issues such as poor health or financial needs. We may face the challenges of growing, maturing or aging. We may even find ourselves in a place where we are following what we feel is God's plan for our lives, but are waiting to hear a word from Him for further direction. We might feel overloaded by the scope of our responsibilities, or that, perhaps, we have let God down, somehow. God may have given us a specific word, and then we become overwhelmed by the scope of His graciousness in wanting to use us. It doesn't matter the situation or scenario life may present, remember this:

- God is always about fulfilling your joy and allowing you to joyfully praise Him wherever you invite Him.
- His loving care is perfect and He has been present all the time.
- God made it possible and is still sustaining what He provided.
- God is there, seen and unseen.
- Trust the God who made you and promised to live within you to guide and secure your present and future.
- It wasn't you in the beginning, so God, who started the blessing, will complete it.
- God cares and He is faithful.
- God chose you and wants you to succeed.
- Wait patiently for God's deliverance.

I could go on and on, giving examples of where God is ever present, but I believe you have gotten the picture. There is no God-free zone in our lives where God will not help us, when asked in faith, believing He is willing and able to deliver. There is no situation, no matter how dark or light, that can exclude God from meeting our needs based on our faith-relationship with Him through Jesus Christ.

Some may ask, "What about sin in our lives?" God has

made it very simple for our sins to be forgiven through our belief in and receiving of Jesus Christ as our Lord and Savior. All we need to do to remove sin is to ask in faith, believing that Christ paid the price for our sin on the cross. Thereby, we establish a relationship with Father God by being a born again child of God and accessible to all His loving promises.

Romans 8:31-39 *What then shall we say to these things? If God is for us, who can be against us? He who did not spare His own Son, but delivered Him up for us all, how shall He not with Him also freely give us all things? Who shall bring a charge against God's elect? It is God who justifies. Who is he who condemns? It is Christ who died, and furthermore is also risen, who is even at the right hand of God, who also makes intercession for us. Who shall separate us from the love of Christ? Shall tribulation, or distress, or persecution, or famine, or nakedness, or peril, or sword? As it is written: "For Your sake we are killed all day long; We are accounted as sheep for the slaughter." Yet in all these things we are more than conquerors through Him who loved us. For I am persuaded that neither death nor life, nor angels nor principalities nor powers, nor things present nor things to come, nor height nor depth, nor any other created thing, shall be able to separate us from the love of God which is in Christ Jesus our Lord.*

There is no hiding place and there is no need to hide from God. He knows us and where we are, and still desires to bless us more than we desire to receive. There is nowhere that God will not meet us and minister His life to us if we invite Him to.

CHAPTER 4
You Purposed Me

Psalm 139:13-16

For You formed my inward parts; You covered me in my mother's womb. I will praise You, for I am fearfully and wonderfully made; Marvelous are Your works, And that my soul knows very well. My frame was not hidden from You, When I was made in secret, And skillfully wrought in the lowest parts of the earth. Your eyes saw my substance, being yet unformed. And in Your book they all were written, The days fashioned for me, When as yet there were none of them.

How many times have you wondered about what your purpose or destiny is in this life? Destiny is defined as: 1) somebody's preordained future, 2) inner realizable purpose of life, or 3) something that predetermines events. There are so many stages or instances in life where we must determine which direction to pursue such as asking what occupation or education level is desired; whether to remain single or marry; how committed to family or Christ will I be? All these questions and decisions focus on your understanding and establishment of your purpose for being.

The enemy and the world system would like us to be convinced that we are the ones, all by ourselves, who determine our destiny. But, once again, according to scripture, we find that God is involved in every endeavor of mankind. The scripture above states that God designed our innermost being. He not only designed us but also constructed us in our mothers' wombs. God desires to be intimately involved in every aspect of our life from beginning to eternity. Let's look at some additional scriptures that describe God's care for His people's destiny:

Isaiah 44:2 *Thus says the Lord who made you And formed you from the womb, who will help you: 'Fear not, O Jacob My servant; And you, Jeshurun, whom I have chosen.*

Isaiah 46:3 *"Listen to Me, O house of Jacob, And all the remnant of the house of Israel, Who have been upheld by Me from birth, Who have been carried from the womb:*

Jeremiah 1:5 *"Before I formed you in the womb I knew you; Before you were born I sanctified you; I ordained you a prophet to the nations."*

In all these scriptures, God is saying that He made us, knowing us even before we were born. In today's terms, we might say that God ordered our DNA and "designer selected" every detail of our being. God has promised to help us and assured us that we need not fear, as His people, because we are chosen. The challenge for God's people is to listen to Him when He speaks words of security and sustaining care which He has given us from birth. Our confidence comes from God affirming His knowledge of each and every one of us. God is not orchestrating His coverage of us by hearsay or sight, but from a supernatural foreknowledge and love that is comprehensive in duration and quantity. God knows what He has done and what we are capable of doing.

When we understand the extent of God's love and devotion to mankind, praise should be our natural reaction followed by love and adoration for God. When we look at the design and masterful construction of the world and mankind, we must confess that we are wonderfully and awe-inspiringly made. Even as man's technology advances, we are not able to duplicate the work of God's hands. Every time we look at ourselves it should cause us to worship, honor, praise, and adore God. We are beings who were created with loving care and attention to details, expressing a level of commitment yet to be fully understood.

Ecclesiastes 11:5 *As you do not know what is the way of the wind, Or how the bones grow in the womb of her who is with child, So you do not know the works of God who makes everything.*

Psalm 90:12 *So teach us to number our days, That we may gain a heart of wisdom.*

We neither know how God did what He did nor does what He does, but we can be confident in knowing that He *did* make everything. Scripture tells us that all the things ordained for our lives, God has written in His book before any of them ever began. In other words, our destiny was written before we were ever born. We are told to number our days or monitor our progress to make sure that we gain a heart of wisdom. God knows what we need and when we need it in order to be successfully pleasing to Him. The question of our lives is will we accept His provision and plan or reject His love. No matter what we choose at the decision points of our lives, we are unable to surprise or upset the intended plan of the loving care and commitment promised by God.

It is critically essential that we, as the people of God, believe that He is not a liar. To believe that what He has said or promised will be backed and enforced by all the power at His disposal. In other words, it *will* be done. Both the Old and New Testaments scriptures report the dependability and veracity of God Almighty toward His word and promises. It is through God's Spirit and word that we have peace that surpasses human understanding and confidence to commit and submit our lives and eternity to Him, joyfully. Take a look at some inspiring and confirming scriptures below.

Numbers 23:19 (NLT) *God is not a man, that he should lie. He is not a human, that he should change his mind. Has he ever spoken and failed to act? Has he ever promised and not carried it through*

Malachi 3:6 *"For I am the Lord, I do not change; Therefore you are not consumed, O sons of Jacob.*

James 1:17 (NLT) *Whatever is good and perfect comes to us from God above, who created all heaven's lights. ^d Unlike them, he never changes or casts shifting shadows.*

Titus 1:2 *in hope of eternal life which God, who cannot lie, promised before time began,*

Hebrews 10:23 *Let us hold fast the confession of our hope without wavering, for He who promised is faithful.*

Proverbs 9:10 *The fear of the Lord is the beginning of wisdom, And the knowledge of the Holy One is understanding.*

The more we know about God and His character, love, righteousness, and holiness, the more we begin to understand just how much we can trust Him. The fear, or reverence, of God that comes from knowing Him, allows us to exercise the knowledge properly, resulting in us possessing wisdom. When we come to understand that God has purposed us and desires to bless us now and throughout eternity, it offers an opportunity to experience the peace and fulfillment ordained for those who love Him. We will begin to see the plan of salvation as the greatest love story ever, with us as the object of God Almighty's divine affection.

To use an analogy regarding tools, God has designed hammers, knives, and screwdrivers for specific uses. Not every tool has the same use, but it is intended to fulfill the purpose for which it was created. You may be able to drive a screw with a knife but not as well or with the endurance of using a screwdriver. When we choose a screwdriver, we find that they are not all the same configuration or even the same size. You may be able to cut something with a screwdriver but it works much better to use a knife. There are also some tools that cannot perform the function of another tool at all; but, there is nothing like having and using the right tool for the right job. Unlike people, we don't hear these tools complaining that they wish they were bigger or that their assigned function would be changed.

We don't know all the details of our future, but the one who loves us best of all does and has ordained a use and blessings for us. As we pursue the plan of God for our lives, we can be assured that we will emerge victoriously as God's highly-favored people. Know that God has purposed you and desires for you to understand your ordained function and position in His kingdom. Celebrate and cherish your God-given purpose and assignment because God has designed you to be successful and fulfilled, pursuing your ordained purpose. When we concentrate more on God's love for us and less on what others are doing compared to us, we will experience the peace and joy promised by God in His Word. Seeking validation from God for our lives is to allow Him to live through us and truly be Lord. What satisfaction can be ours when we realize the originality deposited within us for the fulfillment of God's plan for our life alone. Commitment to the God-established purpose releases us for true greatness and fulfillment.

CHAPTER 5
Precious Are Your Thoughts

Psalm 139:17-18 (NLT)

How precious are your thoughts about me, O God. They cannot be numbered! I can't even count them; they outnumber the grains of sand! And when I wake up, you are still with me!

I believe as David thought about the depth and expanse of God's love for him, he was inspired to write these words in expression of his awe and appreciation for God. God's love had stimulated and, ultimately, encouraged David's love, praise and worship of God as the one who loves us dearly and is the lifter of our heads (Ps. 3:3). It's my contention that a true understanding of God's affection for mankind, and especially those who have accepted His gift in Jesus Christ, will be led also to love, praise, and worship God with all their being.

Take a moment and think about just how much, and in what many ways, God has demonstrated His love and devotion to His people. As you ponder this, with personal examples, you will also declare how precious His thoughts are about you. In realizing that, God has committed to be not only everywhere we are but has promised to take up residence in those of us who receive His son Jesus as Savior. The knowledge and understanding that God thinks about us is to be valued, treasured, and appreciated.

Jeremiah 29:11 *For I know the thoughts that I think toward you, says the Lord, thoughts of peace and not of evil, to give you a future and a hope.*

The book of Jeremiah records some of the thoughts that God had for His people, which are true for us today. God declares that His thoughts are for peace and not evil, with a desire to give us a future and a hope. God has stated that He desires to bless us today and forever. To understand God's thoughts that are recorded in His Word is to comprehend just how much we are valued and need to acknowledge God's loving thoughts toward us. We can never truly and fully comprehend the thoughts and love of God, but we can begin to, at least, confess and admit that we are greatly loved by Him.

One of Satan's main tools of destruction and division is to cause us to think and, finally, believe that God doesn't care about or love us. I am reminded of the words of a song that declares that, "God knows my name". This is birthed in a thought that is derived from understanding that God indeed is intimately familiar with us on a personal-name basis. How many times have we been alienated from other people because we thought they didn't like us or had an issue with something about us? The separation and enmity between us and that person was not resolved until somehow the situation became personal. It's easy to talk down stereotypes and generalities but much harder to put personal interactions and a specifically-named person down. God wants us to know Him because He knows us and cares.

Scripture defines God as love. Now imagine us daring to believe that God is not who He says He is. God built the bridge to gap our separation through the life, death, and resurrection of Jesus Christ. God gave the best that He had, determined to withhold nothing to achieve restoration of mankind to Him. To get a small glimpse of God's unexplainable, unconditional, supernatural, eternity-spanning love is to have peace and experience the reality of true love. Ephesians 2:14 tells us that Jesus, Himself, is our peace. Jesus embodied God's answer to mankind's total need and spiritual deficit.

As we consider God's thoughts about us, we begin to realize that they are beyond counting. It's like trying to think about all the signals that our brain needs to send to our muscles to allow us to walk – there are just too many. Every aspect of our lives and how they are orchestrated with love-infused care by God is overwhelming and overpowering yet comforting to have that sense of guidance and protection being provided supernaturally; to know that no matter what has happened, is happening, or will happen, we are not forgotten or an afterthought. We are ever present in the mind of God and declared precious to Him.

Psalm 40:5 (NLT) *O LORD my God, you have done many miracles for us. Your plans for us are too numerous to list. If I tried to recite all your wonderful deeds, I would never come to the end of them.*

As we examine the word of God in comparison to our lives, we will agree with the psalmist that God has done wonders in our lives. The exciting part of this declaration is that they are things planned for us by God. To know and understand that God is planning growth and blessing for us is comforting and touching. God's attention to detail is so extensive that it doesn't allow full comprehension or expression. We have no need to fear because God has promised to sustain us.

2 Timothy 1:9 (NLT) *It is God who saved us and chose us to live a holy life. He did this not because we deserved it, but because that was his plan long before the world began -- to show his love and kindness to us through Christ Jesus.*

Because we are on the mind of God, He has called us to fellowship and relationship with Him. God, knowing us so well, made provision for our salvation, not based on our performance, but because of His own purpose, operational power, and unmerited favor through Jesus Christ. Note in the scripture above that God's plan and provision was given before the beginning of time. God foreknew us and, according to Scripture, knows the end from the beginning. Think about it; how precious are God's thoughts toward us. It is a love and valuation that exceeds our very capacity to comprehend, resulting in His thoughts and actions being so wonderful and nurturing.

How dear, and to be treasured, is the understanding of God's thoughts toward each of us. Let it never be heard from our mouths that we are not loved and valued as human beings in this life. Our God has promised to never leave us or forsake us; and now to realize that we are ever on His mind with plans to endue us with great fortune, how can we help but worship and adore our Father God.

CHAPTER 6
My Enemies

Psalm 139:19-22

Oh, that You would slay the wicked, O God! Depart from me, therefore, you bloodthirsty men. For they speak against You wickedly; Your enemies take Your name in vain. Do I not hate them, O Lord, who hate You? And do I not loathe those who rise up against You? I hate them with perfect hatred; I count them my enemies

In our desire to serve and appreciate the favor and presence of God, we sometimes become frustrated with the world that surrounds us. The psalmist exclaims, "If only you, God, would slay or remove the wicked away from me," thinking that our greatest temptations and challenges come from outside of us. This is true only if we have not yet, through surrender to the Holy Spirit, dealt with the evil desires and enticements resident within us. As we look at people who have not accepted Christ as their Savior or even some Christians who have not totally surrendered their lives to Christ, we are tempted to think we could better serve God if they were removed from our story's character list. As the psalmist was able to define some of his so-called antagonists, we may, unwittingly, also do the same with those we believe provide us opportunities to stumble.

We sometimes try to pull God into our open dislike of these people, knowing that their actions and obvious lifestyle choices are in opposition to God's Word and His desire for mankind. Holding up to God their abuse of His name and undisguised pursuit of evil, we declare our hatred and abhorrence of these self-labeled and proclaimed sinners. Let us make sure that we truly understand what God desires when we are instructed to hate evil and rebellion. I will explain.

The Psalmist says that he hates those who hate God and declares them to be his enemy. When I looked up the Hebrew definition of "hate," it was defined as having hatred toward one's enemy or foe. The word "enemy," as defined from the Hebrew, means an adversary or foe. So from these definitions it can be understood that these people were working against the plan and purpose of God and were indeed foes to the people of God. As we look deeper into the concept of hatred in the Old and New Testament, we find that what is to be detested or hated is not the person but the sin or behavior displayed by the person. The enemy of the Psalmist and ours is not the person but the sin that is resident and evidenced through their lives.

Let's look at some other scriptures:

Psalm 101:3 *I will set nothing wicked before my eyes; I hate the work of those who fall away; It shall not cling to me.*

In this psalm, David speaks of sin and the worker of sin and declares that he will not look upon anything that is vile. Note that what he hates is the work or what is done. The doers of these evil things are defined as faithless and as those who fall away from God's purpose and plan. This scripture identifies the target or object of our hatred to be activities, not the perpetrators themselves. We can all empathize that, at some point in our lives, we were workers of evil and sin and could be described as faithless (1 Cor. 6:10-11) but praise God, someone shared the Gospel and love of Christ with us; and we became faith-filled disciples of Christ and determined servants of God.

Proverbs 24:17 *Do not rejoice when your enemy falls, And do not let your heart be glad when he stumbles;*

We are instructed to not gloat or rejoice over the calamities that befall our enemies. "You mean that I can't celebrate the defeat of the person who has schemed and connived for my defeat when they are exposed?" No! No, you may not do so and still hope to be found faithful to God's plans and purpose for His people. We must be ever aware that our success and good fortune are a result of God's grace and favor as believers – believers who are committed to doing the will of God consistently.

Matthew 5:43-45 *"You have heard that it was said, 'You shall love your neighbor and hate your enemy.' But I say to you, love your enemies, bless those who curse you, do good to those who hate you, and pray for those who spitefully use you and persecute you, that you may be sons of your Father in heaven; for He makes His sun rise on the evil and on the good, and sends rain on the just and on the unjust.*

In Matthew 5, Jesus addresses the issue of how His disciples are to conduct themselves toward their enemies. Jesus reminds them that they have heard that they were to hate their enemies, but He commands them to love their enemies. Not only are they to love their enemies but to pray for them. To make sure that there was no confusion, Jesus spelled it out and defined the enemies as those who curse, hate, maliciously use, and persecute you; these are the ones we are to love. The end result of our obedience to His command to love is that we will be recognized or identified as the sons of our heavenly Father. Why should we do this? Because God loves them and makes His sun rise and rain fall on the evil and just. God loves people and wants us to do the same. How great an expression of God's love it is to share our most valued possession and knowledge of Jesus Christ as personal Lord and Savior.

We must understand and remember that God is not malicious toward sinners, but He is faithful to His Word. The consequence of sin in our lives produces evil outcomes and death. Just as with the law of gravity, the law of sin works indiscriminately on those who defy it. If you decide to walk off the roof of your home, the law of gravity will pull you to the ground with no personal malice intended. Likewise, when you decide to allow sin to remain in your life, evil will take hold of you and pull you to undesirable destinations of pain and death. The consequences of sin are universal with God, but His pursuit and demonstration of love to believers *and* unbelievers is totally personal.

Luke 6:27, 35-36 *"But to you who are listening I say: Love your enemies, do good to those who hate you, ... But love your* *enemies, do good, and lend, hoping for nothing in return; and your reward will be great, and you will be sons of the Most High. For He is kind to the unthankful and evil. Therefore be merciful, just as your Father also is merciful.*

Jesus wanted us to imitate His Father (who is also now *our* Father), and love by being kind and merciful to those known to be our enemies.

1 Thessalonians 5:15 *See that no one renders evil for evil to anyone, but always pursue what is good both for you and for all.*

We are admonished to not payback wrong for wrong but to endeavor to do good for both others and ourselves. God hates wrong no matter in whom or what it manifests, just as we must.

1 Peter 3:9 *not returning evil for evil or reviling for reviling, but on the contrary blessing, knowing that you were called to this, that you may inherit a blessing.*

We as the people of God are called to be a blessing to others and to be blessed ourselves. As the children of God, our inheritance is that we are blessed now and throughout eternity.

Psalm 23:5 (NLT) *You prepare a feast for me in the presence of my enemies. You honor me by anointing my head with oil. My cup overflows with blessings.*

Because David trusted God and allowed Him to be his shepherd, God blessed David with provision in the presence of his enemies. In Psalm 23, David talks about God's guidance as he walked through life's scary situations but always recognized that his obedience was rewarded with goodness and mercy. David was an example of God's provision for His people right in full view of their enemies' tormented lives. God will use us to make our enemies to desire and know Christ as their Lord when we permit God to love them through us.

We must always remember to hate the sin but love the person. Be followers of Christ and imitators of God's love and mercy. When we ask God for help to be His representatives to the unbelieving world (our enemy), He will deliver empowering, overcoming support.

Isaiah 59:1-2 *Behold, the Lord's hand is not shortened, That it cannot save; Nor His ear heavy, That it cannot hear. But your iniquities have separated you from your God; And your sins have hidden His face from you, So that He will not hear.*

Our enemy is sin found within us. Hate the presence of sin in your life because it will hinder the flow and plan of God for you. As the scripture above indicates, it is not that God's hands are shortened so that He cannot rescue you nor is it that He is hard of hearing. It is our open and *hidden* sins that separate us from God and block the supply lines and communication links between God and us. The issue is unforgiven sin, and yes, rebellion against God's Word. If you are wondering where God is in your situation, check to see if sin is obstructing your deliverance. Trust God to faithfully deliver on His Word. He has promised to forgive when we ask in Jesus' name.

1 John 1:9 *If we confess our sins, He is faithful and just to forgive us our sins and to cleanse us from all unrighteousness.*

CHAPTER 7

Test Me

Psalm 139:23-24

Search me, O God, and know my heart; Try me, and know my anxieties; And see if there is any wicked way in me, And lead me in the way everlasting.

When we have come to the point that we understand that: a) God knows us; b) He has our back; c) we can't hide from Him; d) He purposed us; e) He has precious thoughts of us and; f) He wants us to hate sin, we are then ready to submit to God and participate willingly in His loving relationship that also involves our testing.

The psalmist, at the end of his declaration, requested that God search him. This, to many of us, sounds strange and maybe even masochistic. The implications of David's understanding of and devotion to God are made clear in this avowed desire to be tested. David wanted God to search and test him to know his often hidden or denied concerns, worries, and apprehensions. Since God already knew David, it was an exercise designed to reveal to David, himself, his inner thoughts and fears. If we would admit it, we would confess that we have concealed concerns about ourselves that produce restlessness in our hearts and minds, even in the face of God's promise to provide peace and sanctuary.

Deuteronomy 8:2-3 *And you shall remember that the Lord your God led you all the way these forty years in the wilderness, to humble you and test you, to know what was in your heart, whether you would keep His commandments or not. So He humbled you, allowed you to hunger, and fed you with manna which you did not know nor did your fathers know, that He might make you know that man shall not live by bread alone; but man lives by every word that proceeds from the mouth of the Lord.*

Moses, in this Scripture, was warning the Israelites regarding their relationship with God before they were to enter the Promised Land. Moses challenged them to remember the acts of God over the past forty years and how He had humbled them, tested them and yet met their needs. The word used for humble here means to abase, afflict, chasten, deal hardly with, and exercise. As we read about the forty years in the wilderness, we can see God's exercise of humility on His people and continual testing of their obedience. The purpose of the humbling and testing was to reveal to the Israelites the true condition of their hearts and commitment to obey. God already knew that they were lost without Him, but He wanted them to recognize and acknowledge the facts for themselves and seek His help. God was teaching them that His Word is the source of life for all mankind and available through His love.

1 Peter 5:6-7 (NLT) *So humble yourselves under the mighty power of God, and in his good time he will honor you. Give all your* *worries and cares to God, for he cares about what happens to you.*

When we comprehend and embrace God's love and plan for our lives and compare that with our experience, it will causes us to ask, "Is there something offensive to God in me?" We ask this of ourselves because we know there is no failure or deficiency in God but plenty that can be improved in us. Trusting in the promises of God, we are willing to submit to examination and the necessary humbling, repair process. We may ask why God loves us the way He does, but there is no other answer than that it's just who God is—Love. It is a love that Paul asked, "Who can separate us from the love of Christ?"(Rom. 8:35) The answer that should echo through our minds and hearts is a resounding, "NO one or NO thing."

As the child who allows his father to throw him into the air, all the while laughing and squealing with delight, we must trust our Father God to faithfully catch and protect us. Just a glimpse of the commitment and pledged devotion of God stimulates our desire to serve, worship, and obey Him. If we truly want help, we must be willing to expose ourselves through admitting and confessing what God's Word says about us. If you are sinning, then confess it and allow God to forgive you, and then also confess that you are forgiven and blessed forever and ever because God said so. Run to God knowing that He already knows your faults and *still* desires to forgive when asked to in Jesus' name.

Yes, ask God to search and test you knowing that whatever is revealed and surrendered will be handled with loving care. We should be able to, as David could, cast our cares and burdens on Christ believing that He cares for us. When we trust the heart of God, we can submit our very essence into His care and stewardship. We can have faith that He values and desires to minister abundant life and eternal salvation to us. Doubt and fear are the enemy of faith, and it is only through faith in God that we will ever be able to please Him.

Let's look at what some other scriptures say regarding allowing God to examine our lives.

Job 31:6 *Let me be weighed on honest scales, That God may know my integrity.*

Job trusted God to review his case believing that He would do right by him and support him in his time of difficulty. Job understood that there was no hiding from God's presence and therefore His influence. Job spoke to God, knowing He was listening and cared even though he didn't know the whys or reasoning for his predicament. Job ran to God, not away from Him, knowing God could fix the hurt.

Psalm 5:8 *Lead me, O Lord, in Your righteousness because of my enemies; Make Your way straight before my face.*

We must, as David did, desire to be lead by God. Our righteousness, of necessity, is to be God's righteousness and not our own. Our righteousness is insufficient to stand in the face of our enemies who plan our destruction and downfall. David requested that the Lord make his way straight or honest before his face. We need to allow God's Word to speak to us, and the Spirit of God to provide the understanding that will promote our obedience and integrity of character. Our declaration should be "Make it plain, Father."

Psalm 143:10 *Teach me to do Your will, For You are my God; Your Spirit is good. Lead me in the land of uprightness.*

In order for God to teach us through His will and Word, we need to discern His spirit and presence. We must submit to examination and life-testing to progress toward the image of Christ, our perfect example.

1 Samuel 16:7 *But the Lord said to Samuel, "Do not look at his appearance or at his physical stature, because I have refused him. For the Lord does not see as man sees; for man looks at the outward appearance, but the Lord looks at the heart."*

To submit to God's arena of testing is to know that He is not looking at our superficial, exhibited façade. God looks where others, in the natural, have difficulty or are incapable of observing, but it is the only place that truly counts to Him – our heart. It is the heart that will drive and orchestrate a person's behavior.

Proverbs 17:3 *The refining pot is for silver and the furnace for gold, But the Lord tests the hearts.*

God tests our hearts to reveal to us that we need even more work than we thought or would consciously admit. Our admission or confession is what God desires along with our invitation for His loving intervention.

1 Corinthians 10:13 *No temptation has overtaken you except such as is common to man; but God is faithful, who will not allow you to be tempted beyond what you are able, but with the temptation will also make the way of escape, that you may be able to bear it.*

This scripture should encourage us to believe that in His testing or in the middle of temptations which may come from the enemy, God does not allow or endorse destructive testing. God is involved and interested in every individual in humanity. He will always provide a means of escape or victory for *His* ordained testing. It is our choice to choose God's deliverance or Satan's destructive route or venue.

James 1:13-14 *Let no one say when he is tempted, "I am tempted by God"; for God cannot be tempted by evil, nor does He Himself tempt anyone. But each one is tempted when he is drawn away by his own desires and enticed.*

God's test will challenge us to do good things and improve our ability to serve righteously. God will never entice or test us with evil; that's Satan's practice. God will always provide opportunities to grow and advance our understanding of Him and ourselves, opportunities that will produce life and not destruction. We can safely trust God to endorse testing that benefits us and draws us closer to Him. God's challenges will always prepare us to face, victoriously, the evil temptations offered by Satan.

So say boldly with David, "Test me." Trust God to be everywhere and everything you need when you need it.

CHAPTER 8
Living in God's Presence

Hebrews 13:5-6

Let your conduct be without covetousness; be content with such things as you have. For He Himself has said, "I will never leave you nor forsake you." So we may boldly say: "The Lord is my helper; I will not fear. What can man do to me?"

At this point in our discussion of there being no God-free zone, you, hopefully, have come to an understanding of the benefits and desirability of the loving presence of God in your life. There should be no question that God, through Jesus Christ and the Holy Spirit, yearns to be involved in every aspect of your life both now and throughout eternity. It is our understanding, and subsequent embracing of God's doting, affectionate presence, that allows us to cherish His attention and invest our lives in worship and service to Him. The more we appreciate, trust, and depend upon our relationship with God, the more access and realization we are given to the promises of security and provision afforded in His comprehensive salvation gift. Acceptance of God's gift allows Him to cover and wrap us in His love, grace, and righteousness.

We often hear other Christians talk about "the presence

of God." Sometimes they will invite the presence of God as if He is not *always* attending to us, and is living somewhere outside of us as believers. To use an analogy regarding God's presence, we can look at the air or atmosphere we breathe to live. The atmosphere is everywhere and it sustains life; but when people ask for tangible evidence of God's presence, it's like asking for a breeze to blow. Just as the air we breathe is there all around us, it is so refreshing to have a cool breeze blow on a hot day. The tangible presence of God reassures us of the relationship that does, and always must, exist to support life. But without the knowledge of God's existence and vowed attendance, we are unable to recognize His communication. That is why it is so important that we study and come to understand God's intention of inseparable commitment left to us in His Word.

God is ever present and wants us to acknowledge His presence whether we can sense Him or not. God has told us that without faith it is impossible to please Him (Hebrews 11:6). As promised, God is always present but when we focus our attention on Him, we become *conscious* of His continual attendance. In order to please God, we must believe that He is, and that He desires to reward us for our faith in Him. It will always be the *belief* that God is there, more than just our sensory feedback. That belief is what will produce the greatest manifestations of God's presence and intervention for mankind. Yes, we need to see the power of God manifested in our lives, but it is our faith in Him that produces the results and not our need. Until we believe that He who has promised is faithful and ever present, we will experience the unnecessary fear and torment never intended by God for His people.

In the scripture above, we are admonished to keep our lives free from the love of money and this statement can be cross-referenced with Luke 12:15, *And He said to them, "Take heed and beware of covetousness, for one's life does not consist in the abundance of the things he possesses."* The parable includes a warning for those who store up things for themselves but are not rich toward God. Greed can be directed or focused on all kinds of things. These *things*, by themselves, can be productive when properly utilized. To be rich toward God is to invest our lives in the acceptance of His gift of salvation and covering presence. Our focus in life is to grow and nurture our bond with God through Jesus Christ. Dare to get to know Him and His abiding presence through an ever-increasing, faith-building love relationship.

Once we truly have Christ in our lives as Lord and Savior, then we can sincerely be content with what we have. To know that we are loved, bonded, affiliated with, and valued by the God of the universe is indeed true contentment. According to 1 Timothy 6:6 (KJV), "But godliness with contentment is great gain". Being content with God's presence in our lives, and allowing Him to change and affect how we live – which is to be described as godly or holy – is eternally priceless. Then we can be confident when God promises to never leave or forsake us. What a promise from an ever- faithful God!

God has made Himself known to us so that we may have

confidence through Him to conquer our everyday life experiences. God's desire is that we will experience for ourselves, and then boldly declare to Him and anyone He sends across our path, that He is our helper and He loves us. First John 4:18 (NLT) tells us that, *Such love has no fear because perfect love expels all fear. If we are afraid, it is for fear of judgment, and this shows that his love has not been perfected in us.* It is God's love that assures His presence and commitment to us. Let's allow His love to drive any fear far from us and allow His perfecting love to grow in us day by day and from grace to grace. That grace is the operational power of God and His unmerited favor and kindness.

Here are the seven steps to understanding the presence of God found in Psalms 139:

1. Settle in your heart that God knows you.
2. Realize God has your interest at heart; He's got your back.
3. Accept that there is no hiding from God.
4. Appreciate that God has purposed you and your life.
5. Embrace the fact that God thinks you are precious and valuable.
6. Make God's enemy your enemy.
7. Trust God enough to submit to His testing.

Look for each of these steps in the lives of God's people in the Bible, and allow them to become an integral part of your life; then more and more, from faith to faith, your understanding of the overwhelming presence of God will continue to expand until you see Him face-to-face.

Numbers 23:19-20 (NLT) *God is not a man, that he should lie. He is not a human, that he should change his mind. Has he ever spoken and failed to act? Has he ever promised and not carried it through. I received a command to bless; he has blessed, and I cannot reverse it!*

In this scripture Balaam, an evil prophet, is encouraged to curse the people of God. Balaam's response to his sponsor is that he cannot curse those whom the Lord has blessed. Balaam states that God is not a man that He should lie or change His mind but will speak and then act. Balaam was instructed by God to declare a blessing that was already spoken by Him over Israel.

God has declared in Hebrews 13:5-6 that He will never leave His people or forsake them. God cannot and will not lie; there is no one who can change His mind. We may change ours, but He will faithfully be there when we decide to return. God will be unchanged in His covenant of love and devotion.

Declare with boldness and confidence, "I will not fear because God is my helper, my colleague, my partner, and my coworker." Understand the meaning of the presence of God and know with certainty that there is "No God-free Zone" for those in Christ Jesus. God has spoken and is performing His word!

www.ingramcontent.com/pod-product-compliance
Lightning Source LLC
Chambersburg PA
CBHW031429290426
44110CB00011B/594